Eggs

Edited by Rebecca Stefoff

Text © 1991 by Garrett Educational Corporation

First Published in the United States in 1991
by Garrett Educational Corporation,
130 East 13th, Ada, Oklahoma 74820

First Published in 1990 by A & C Black (Publishers) Limited, London
with the title EGGS
© 1990 A & C Black (Publishers) Ltd.

Manufactured in the United States of America

Library of Congress Cataloging in Publication Data

Moss, Miriam.
     Eggs / Miriam Moss.
     p.   cm.—(Threads)
     Summary: Discusses eggs, their sources, their uses for food and fun,
and presents recipes and activities with eggs.
     ISBN 1-56074-005-1 : $15.93
     1. Eggs—Juvenile literature.   2. Cookery (Eggs)—Juvenile literature.
[1. Eggs.]   I. Title.   II. Series.
SF490.3.M67   1991
637'.5—dc20   91-18186
                                                              CIP
                                                              AC

Eggs

Miriam Moss

Photographs by Robert Pickett

Contents

GEC GARRETT EDUCATIONAL CORPORATION

Different kinds of birds' eggs

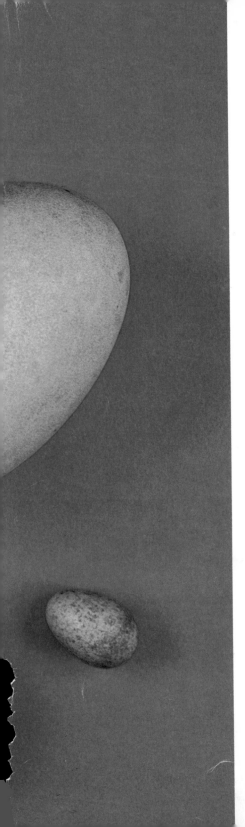

Can you match these birds with their eggs on the opposite page? (The answers are on page 25.)

Robin

Herring gull

Tawny owl

Goose

Hen

Birds are all sorts of different shapes, sizes and colors — so are their eggs. Try and describe the shapes of these eggs.

Most of the eggs we eat come from hens, like this bird.

What's inside an egg?

Only female birds can lay eggs. If a female bird has mated with a male bird before she lays her eggs, a baby bird may start to grow inside each egg. These eggs are called fertilized eggs.

The eggs we eat are laid by female birds that have not mated with a male bird. They are called unfertilized eggs and they do not have baby birds growing inside them.

An egg is a perfect home for a growing chick. You can see this by looking inside an unfertilized egg.

Crack open an egg into ▶ a saucer. Gently touch the yellow center, called the yolk. Can you feel some skin? This skin separates the yolk from the white.

What does egg white ▶ feel like? Can you see any twisted bundles of egg white? These hold the yolk away from the shell so that when the egg rolls, the yolk stays in the middle of the egg.

4

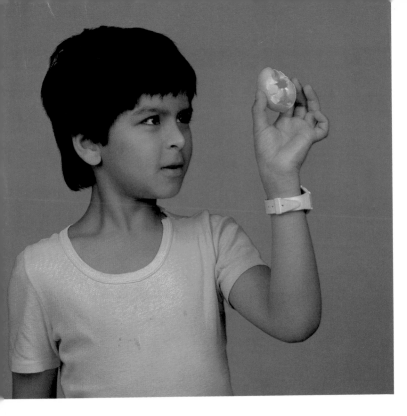

◀ Hold some eggshell to the light. Can you see lots of tiny holes? These let air into the egg. The chick needs air to grow.

▲

The eggshell is stuck to a strong, papery white skin. Peel off some skin. How stretchy is it? Leave the skin to dry for five minutes. How stretchy is it now?

◀ Wiggle your finger about in the round end of the eggshell. What does the papery skin feel like here? This is where there is a pocket of air between the skin and the shell.

Chicken and egg

These pictures show a chick growing inside a fertilized egg.

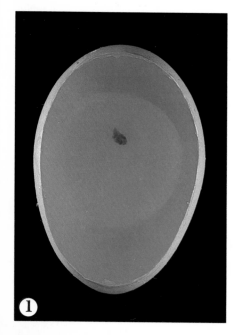

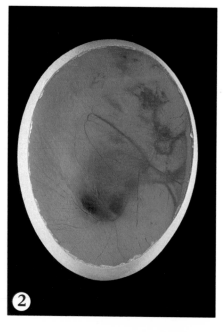

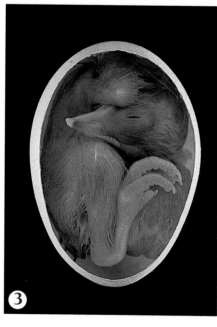

1. This hen's egg was laid one day ago. The red dot on the yolk is called a germ cell. It will grow into a chick.

2. For ten days, the hen has been sitting on the egg, keeping it warm and safe. The chick is growing inside a bag of water, called a sac. The sac protects the chick from damage. Narrow red blood vessels carry food and air to the growing chick.

3. In this photograph, the sac around the chick has been removed to show you what the chick looks like after three weeks. The chick cheeps — it is ready to hatch.

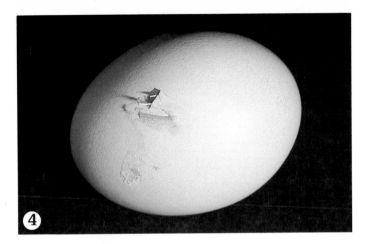

4. The chick cracks the hard shell with the eggtooth on the end of its beak. Under the shell is a layer of papery white skin, which keeps the chick moist and free from germs. It's the same as the stretchy skin you looked at on page 5.

5. The chick struggles out of the egg and will need to rest before it stands up. Its feathers are wet and shiny.

Birds are not the only animals that lay eggs. Insects, fish, and reptiles also hatch out of eggs. Find out some more about the eggs of these animals.

Why are eggs egg-shaped?

What happens when you roll an uncooked egg on the floor?

Eggs are specially shaped to roll in a curve, back to the center of the birds' nest.

How strong is an egg?

Make you thumb and first finger into the shape of the letter C. Now pick up an egg with its rounded end at the bottom. You can squeeze the egg quite hard before it breaks.

An egg is a strong shape that can support a lot of weight. Tiny bits of shell, called crystals, rest against each other like the bricks in an arch.

On your way to school, see how many egg-shapes and half egg-shapes you can find in buildings.

Can you see any eggs on this stony beach? Often eggs are difficult to see because they blend into their surroundings. They are camouflaged from animals who might want to eat them.

Some birds that nest in bushes lay speckled green eggs, which are difficult to spot against their nests and the bushes. Many birds' eggs are white because they are hidden by the parent bird sitting on them.

Some birds build nests and sit on their eggs until the chicks are ready to hatch. But this blue-footed boobie keeps its eggs warm on its feet. Can you think of another bird that does this?

Eggs for eating

At the battery egg farm

Most of the eggs we buy in shops come from hens kept on large battery farms. The hens live inside cages and never go outside. Four birds live inside each cage. The hens eat a mixture of grains from a conveyor belt. They drink water from small taps inside their cages.

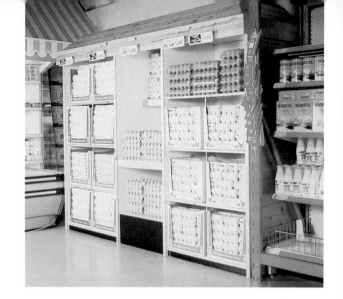

The hens lay one egg a day. The eggs roll on to a conveyor belt which travels to a machine that carefully moves the eggs on rollers. These women take out any cracked or dirty eggs before the machine puts the eggs on to large trays.

The trays are stacked on a trolley and stored in a big refrigerator, until they are taken to the packing station.

11

At the free-range egg farm

Some people prefer to buy eggs which come from free-range hens. These eggs are called free-range eggs, and they cost a bit more than eggs that come from battery hens.

During the day, free-range hens can wander in a field. At night, they are kept inside a hen-house, out of the cold and away from foxes. The hens are fed and watered inside.

The hens lay their eggs in nesting-boxes at the back of the hen-house. The eggs roll through a flap to a bench outside, where the are collected twice a d

At the packing station

Newly laid free-range and battery eggs are taken by truck to the packing station. The eggs are passed under lights, which show up any cracks in their shells. This is called candling because the eggs were once checked by candlelight.

Any cracked or broken eggs are used to make paint, soap, shampoo, ink and fertilizer.

Next, the eggs are sorted into sizes. Several sizes of egg are sold in the grocery stores. Jumbo is the biggest. What size egg do you usually eat?

Six or twelve eggs are packed into each egg-box. The box holds the eggs safely in place so that they won't break.

Each box is date-stamped to show how fresh the eggs are. It takes only one or two days for an egg to get from the hen to the supermarket.

Fresh and stale eggs

Do you know how to tell if an egg is fresh or stale?

How to do it

Gently lower the egg into the jam jar. Does it float or does it sink?

As an egg gets older, it slowly loses water, which is heavy. Also, air gets into the egg through the tiny holes in its shell. This air makes the air space at the rounded end of the egg get bigger. A stale egg floats because it is light and contains more air than a fresh egg.

Is the egg in the jam jar on the left fresh or stale?

You will need

An egg

A jam jar of water

Eggs keep fresh in the refrigerator for up to three weeks. Store them away from strong-smelling food. The smell can pass into an egg through the tiny holes in its shell.

15

Eggs for special occasions

All over the world, eggs are used in customs that celebrate birth. In China, when a baby is born, its family paints eggs red, which is the color of happiness. This is to give the baby good luck. You can make your own happiness eggs by painting eggs red.

At Muslim weddings, specially wrapped eggs are given to the wedding couple, to wish them healthy children.

A Chinese egg legend

This Chinese legend tells the story of how the world was created from an egg.

Pan Gu Lay was a giant who lived inside a huge egg. The egg was the universe.

One day, as Pan Gu Lay was resting, a crack appeared on the shell of the egg. Then gradually more and more cracks appeared. Pan Gu Lay gave a mighty push and broke free from the egg. Jagged pieces of shell scattered far and wide. The broken bits of eggshell became the sea, sky and earth.

For thousands of years, eggs have been used in festivals that celebrate the arrival of spring, the flowering of plants, and birth of animals.

The springtime custom of giving eggs as presents also became popular at Easter. Easter is a Christian festival, which celebrates the story of Christ's rebirth. On Good Friday, Christ was killed on a cross, but on the following Sunday he rose from the dead. Nowadays, decorated or chocolate Easter eggs are given on Easter Sunday.

Decorated hard-boiled eggs make good presents. Try to make an egg look like a friend or a clown. Draw or paint on the face and then stick on wool for hair and make cardboard hats and ears.

In the nineteenth century, a famous Russian jeweler named Carl Fabergé decorated hollow eggs with jewels. Inside each egg, there was a beautiful surprise present. You can make your own Fabergé egg by sticking sequins, glitter, and brightly colored beads on to an egg.

There is an old English custom of giving patterned eggs at Easter. They are called pace eggs.

How to make an English pace egg

You will need

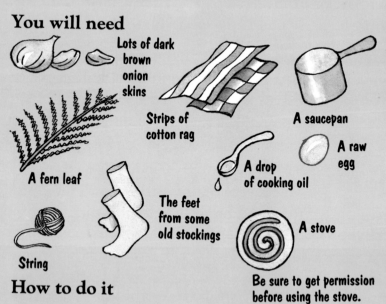

Lots of dark brown onion skins

A fern leaf

Strips of cotton rag

A saucepan

A drop of cooking oil

A raw egg

String

The feet from some old stockings

A stove

Be sure to get permission before using the stove.

How to do it

1. Wrap a fern leaf around the egg. Then wrap the egg in several layers of onion skins. Hold these in place by wrapping cotton rags around the egg.

Put the egg into the foot of a pair of stockings and tie up the end securely with string.

2. Ask an adult to help you gently lower the egg into a saucepan of water. Boil the egg for 30 minutes. Leave the water to cool before removing the egg. Take the layers of stockings, rag, onion skin, and fern leaf away.

3. Rub some cooking oil into the egg to make the golden pattern shiny.

①

②

③

Eggs in our food

Eggs can be cooked in many different ways. What's your favorite way of eating eggs?

Custard

Egg yolks thicken soups and sauces, and are used to make mayonnaise.

Chocolate mousse

Mayonnaise

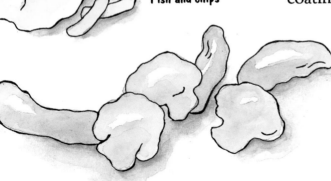
Fritters

Fish and chips

Eggs bind food together and can make cripsy coatings.

Hamburgers

Tempura

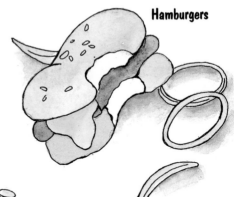

Egg whites make food light and airy.

Egg-fried rice

Meringues

It's best to eat well-cooked eggs. Babies, pregnant women, and people who are old or ill should avoid uncooked or lightly cooked eggs. They might cause food poisoning.

Sweet eggs

Try making a sandwich cake

You will need

2 large eggs

4 oz. self-raising flour

1 teaspoon baking powder

2 drops of vanilla essence

4 oz. confectioner's sugar

4 oz. soft margarine

Jam for the filling

A wooden spoon

A strainer

2 greased baking pans

A wire rack

A knife

A large mixing bowl

Set the oven to 375°F

Oven gloves

How to do it

①

1. Strain the flour and baking powder into a large mixing bowl. Add the sugar and stir it all up.

②

2. Crack the eggs into the mixture. Add the vanilla essence and margarine. Beat the mixture hard with a wooden spoon, until it is soft and pale.

3. Pour half the mixture into one greased pan and half into the other. Smooth down the mixture in each pan with the back of the spoon.

4. Bake the cakes in the oven for about 30 minutes, until they look golden brown. Ask an adult to help you take them out of the oven. Carefully turn the cakes out of the pans and cool on a wire rack.

5. Spread jam on the flat side of each cake and sandwich them together. Sprinkle confectioner's sugar on the top.

Perhaps your friends would like a slice?

Indian eggs

Try making this egg dish that comes from South India. It's called eggs pulusu.

You will need

Mix 1 teaspoon each of ground cumin, ground coriander seeds and turmeric

A pinch of salt

1 tablespoon of tomato purée

A chopped onion

1 cup water

4 large hard-boiled eggs, sliced in half

3 tablespoons vegetable oil

A wooden spoon

A frying pan and lid

A stove

How to do it

①

1. Ask an adult to help you gently heat the oil in the frying pan. Fry the onion until you can almost see through it. Stir in the spice mixture and cook for a minute. Add the tomato purée and salt, and cook for another minute.

②

2. Carefully add the water. Give the mixture a good stir and cover with a lid. Simmer on a low heat for 2-3 minutes.

③

3. Add the eggs, yolk-side up. Spoon some of the sauce over the eggs and cook for about 3 minutes. Serve with rice or slices of buttered toast.

More things to do

1. Try this simple way of decorating eggs. Paint a pattern on an egg with lemon juice. Then boil the egg in a large saucepan of water with beetroot peelings. The beetroot will dye the egg except where you painted it with the lemon juice.

2. Do you know how to tell if an egg is hard-boiled or not? A hard-boiled egg spins on its rounded end and an uncooked one doesn't. Try this for yourself.

3. Eggs are good for you. They contain protein, minerals and carbohydrates. Over a week, keep a diary of how many eggs you eat.

4. How to blow an egg: With a pin, gently make a small hole in the top of an egg. Make another small hole at the other end of the egg. Now hold the egg over a bowl and blow through one of the holes. The inside of the egg will come out of the other end. Carefully wash the egg in some soapy water, then rinse it under a trickle of water from the tap and leave to dry. Decorate your blown egg, but be careful: it is very fragile.

5. Find out what pickled eggs taste like.

6. Do you know the saying, "Don't put all your eggs in one basket"? Can you think of any more sayings about eggs and chickens?

7. The best way to separate an egg yolk from egg white is to break the egg on to a saucer and then to cover the yolk with an egg cup. Hold the egg cup firmly over the yolk and pour the white into a bowl. Try this yourself.

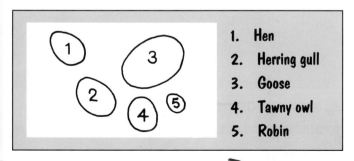

1. Hen
2. Herring gull
3. Goose
4. Tawny owl
5. Robin

Index